cloudraker

POETRY MEMOIR   HEATHER GRACE

All proceeds of book sales are donated to
www.wordoflifewellness.org

ARCHWAY
PUBLISHING

Archway Publishing books may be ordered through booksellers or by contacting:

Archway Publishing
1663 Liberty Drive
Bloomington, IN 47403
www.archwaypublishing.com
844-669-3957

ISBN: 978-1-4808-7662-0 (sc)
ISBN: 978-1-4808-7663-7 (hc)
ISBN: 978-1-4808-7661-3 (e)

Library of Congress Control Number: 2019908095

Print information available on the last page.

Archway Publishing rev. date: 06/10/2021

This complexity

I distilled

in four sentences,

or better yet

one sentence,

was going to run a river of ink to people I would

never meet.

Just Start

Let's begin each day again,
all of us.

Except me.

I don't want to get out of bed.

I hope my words make someone feel something.

If not, that's okay.

Some of us don't feel too well.

In all of it, God remains
whom I sprint to
for comfort.

Usually when things are going horribly wrong.

I am intensely private

now, let my tears and my laughter

be carried to you in words.

I saw little dots as I lay on my back,

birds so far away,

sun sparkling through leaves.

It was my first memory …

Or maybe I just made it up.

………………

They had conversations I did not understand.

I wanted to walk like they did.

Talk their language.

Yet all I could do was crawl.

Mom

You are the toughest woman I know.

You taught me to make it alone.

I often felt lonely.

Now solitude is my sanctuary.

*P.S. I did write a letter to ask to go live with the
neighbor when I was seven.*

. . . .

Fights and tears,

Snow and flowers,

Screams and fears,

Orchards and swings:

We were just farm kids trapped in barefoot games.

Adults there, but not really there.

She sat cuddling her newborn

with pride and adoration in a Kodak 35mm photo.

The love intention was there.

Did not exactly turn into a fairy tale

or a nightmare—

was something in between.

....

She arrived at our doorstep.

Raped.

Naked.

You took your clothes off immediately

and covered her.

My selfless mother.

Watching Mom and Dad,

I guess with your dope and her drinking,

your constant obsession with sex,

there was no space for a conversation about love.

That violet bruise on your face you tried to wash away with wine.

While other women used lies and foundation, you just drowned in red, listening to blues.

Boarding school was a relief—
quiet,
no chores.

I sometimes politely asked to stay there on
weekends.

....

How did you wipe five noses,
feed five mouths?
You always helped me.
Me?
So small I can't even remember.

Don't forget: we also had to clip one hundred nails
and toenails.

TEENY MOMMA

Was I ever really a teen?

Or did I go straight to baby adult?

He watched me walk across the restaurant.

He ordered a drink.

He put a tip in my top.

He touched my breast.

I was poor—gave him back the note.

Saying, "I am not for sale," made me rich.

Thirteen

Her gentle silk threads

intertwined

in a whirlwind of chaos and grit.

....

North was south.

West was east.

The search for my moral compass happened

far too late.

Mom, all I want is a "sorry."

All those memories locked in a long time ago.

Even if I scratch the topic,

All I get is a growl.

Just say, "I blacked out a lot."

That's enough sorry for a lifetime of drunk.

Dad, you gave me bipolar, apparently.

What an unlucky generational gift.

Out of all your children, why me?

....

You were in agony, sobbing,

Begging me not to tell anyone.

I was too little for such a large secret.

Bona Fide Shrink at Four

And all that makeup sex.

You confused her.

So she sat for many nights, listening to Leonard

Cohen to try to grasp you.

Not much to grasp about an erection.

Hypersexual

Your sister fell off a horse and crushed her neck.

She died.

Then you died inside.

So you tried to feel by beating women.

Then you tattooed a horse on your heart.

Dad's hairy chest.

....

You bought her flowering plants when she

bore your children:

the first, the second, the fifth.

You wanted twelve.

You also punched her down the stairs.

I thought you'd broken your arm,

when I heard that something was wrong with you.

Instead, you were dead.

You shot yourself through that horse on your heart.

Clever moving target. No practice needed.

God was there.

I felt Him.

At your funeral, and I hated Him.

Much later, He came back and said, "Hello."

Now we are talking again.

. . . .

I came out of the washing machine

that was on spin cycle

with sharp stones.

I had scars.

Ended up scarred and kind.

You were left with five. All so small, so needy,

clutching at your breasts

while you smelled of white wine and sweat.

Everything seemed okay to everyone

on the outside,

but it was filthy inside.

We needed a cleaner in our childhood home.

Now I understand you, Mom,

because she overwhelms me.

Sometimes, I smell like booze.

I grab her out of her bed in the middle of the night
for a hug, smelling like the bar I was in.

She does not want to come near me because
of the stink.

I went back,

saw the mountains,

the blue country sky,

everything I missed as a teenager.

I was always working, trying to avoid going home,

or somewhere getting to second base with boys.

Twenty Years Later

Never!

Just in case suicide does not work.

I don't want to be the girl who was meant
to be dead.

I will hold onto hope, the hope you lost.

I will hold onto it for you Dad.

I was always
interested
in the misfits.

Comfortable between
normal and absurd.

Trying to Be
An Adult

Writing is an
effortless
escape—

also excruciating

as blank pages stare at me
in between birthing poems.

I was like you for a few years,

abusing sex and drugs—

one brilliant thrill mirror.

Loved every moment, but had to stop. *Sigh.*

Predator

I prowled and mounted.
"Leave before dawn," I said.
I discarded them without coffee or breakfast.
They obliged—many, many of them.

....

He knew my hip to waist ratio,
called me his golden unicorn.

Such a delicious snack.

"I want you."

Men like to hear that.

We go back to mine, and it's not fun because it's a
game,

a game that leaves me empty, going out,

chasing more emptiness.

....

This is not normal, she said.

To be so impulsive.

To be so sexual.

To be so reckless.

She diagnosed me.

I resented being a template in a book.

I wish one of you had been there
in the times when I was floored,
when I needed someone to hug me, since I had no
idea what was happening to my mind.

....

He was crushing on me.
Wanted to read my writing.
It makes me sound a bit disturbed.
I can handle that, he said.
When it's in black and white, it's very real.
He looked at me, suddenly afraid.

Please Don't

How many times have I had to wake up to

"I really like you,"

and my head begs,

please tell me you got carried away,

you were drunk,

you romanticized.

Anything but "I really like you."

Soon you will be thinking "I love you."

Just go away with that.

I've had micro lovers.

I've had macro lovers.

They were all equal lovers.

Size should never matter—not his or hers.

All these lies about kissing

The fairytales
The movies
The songs

They all have THE KISS

Don't you know kissing strangers can give you
herpes?

....

I saw you across a room,
and I knew instantly I wanted to be part of your
tower.
I walked across and told you that.
You blushed.
A crimson man.

We wrote and shared poetry.

I told you if we were friends,

we could never be lovers.

You tried it on me,

so I left

with all your poems.

Score.

I found drugs
so much easier to get high,
quicker than lying there, waiting for him to orgasm.

What was your name again?

I decided to change.

I was using the wrong medication.

Sex and pills or powder.

Gratitude is the soft lavender

you can always smell in your life.

Except when you stand in shit.

You will have to wash that off first.

Be exceptionally mad but exquisitely kind.

I wrote
about the madly delicious spirals,
the

Ascents,

God,

Dysfunction,

Delight.

So many unfinished journals.

You,

on the floor.

I don't know what it was,

I did not know you, but I wanted

to lie on your chest.

You gave me a card that said, "I love you."

The words were scratched out with a marker;

Instead, it said, "I like you."

The best valentine.

The only one I wanted.

I dropped in love.

Fell would have been too soft.

The most

delicious,

magnificent,

delicate,

divine

drop in the world.

....

Your dark brain

matches mine.

Will we hurt too much together,

or laugh until we lose our minds?

He said, "Celebrate."

So I jumped into the crowd.

Twice.

Could have broken my neck.

A crowd of twenty at a failed rock concert.

....

We were magnets.

I tried to stay away.

I kept getting stuck

to you.

So cold,

So hard,

So damn attractive.

You called me before your wedding

and said you were making a mistake.

You wanted me,

but not enough.

You were the longest it ever took me to remove

myself from a love-trap-wrap.

Simple sounds around me
struck me like sickening screams.
I wanted a quiet room,
surrounded by nothing.

And some cocaine—that's a good idea.

Isolated

Women:

Deliberate.
Delicate.
Powerful.
Passionate.

You glue me together.

Ten Years

What was it about him that you loved?

I forget.

It's been 15 years.

....

Marriage

Should be glued using

Love

Respect

Friendship

Laughter

Togetherness.

Mine was glued with trauma.

Trauma-based love

is the most fascinating

love of them all.

You don't know

why you are doing it.

The world thinks

you are mad.

So you start secrets.

Half truths

keeping the whole to yourself.

You think you know better.

That you will heal and cure,

with a perseverance

the world lacks.

It's pitiful and laughable.

My most severe trauma

repeated for years.

Seeing a text:

"Please call me"

I knew I'd be receiving

a smashed package

wrecked by coke

and cheap spirits.

. . . .

Part hate, part love would talk to me.

I knew he wanted to be held,

fixed up and dragged away from

a 2-star hotel, with

crack pipes and condoms.

To our home.

Where spirits were high and pipes banned.

I would try to make everything ok.

Hold down his 180-pound body.

That would sometimes thrash

like there was a devil inside.

I'd manage to get a sleeping tablet in

using vodka and once dodging a knife.

Refusing to think I was ever the victim

of physical abuse.

I was trying to make everything ok.

. . . .

Please call me.

Please call me.

Please call me.

Please call me.

It became the beat

of a life, a love,

a husband.

I got us a place.

Trying to make him stop.

Then he started hating on me.

There was always paranoia,

an agenda that I was there

to steal his last, cheat, betray.

Betray this strong layered love

we had.

....

"Have you been verbally abused?"

No—my first response.

Your first response is the language,

the one you were born into.

No—my first response.

While being pulverized

Each mouth beating

Giving me more

Indignation

That I could conquer

This.

For US of course.

This went on until he bound me

Sharing the glass pipe

He knew I was the next shelter

Warmer than motels

With working girls

That my arms would care,

a nurse looking to cure

the memories of the past

by fixing his despair.

I was not even co-dependent.

I was enmeshed.

I was raging,

fury,

often tired and wishing for a moment

he would die.

10 years

I lived through it

8 months white knuckling it

Spewing rehab talk to me

Me believing this moment

Was different. Then again:

White knuckles,

New fists of denial

Geography, spirituality, a new loan, a new town, a
new game, a new car, a new day, a new hour, a new
bed, new linen, new clothes, new shoes, new bail,
old jail, new time.
Each "new"
a hope that the old new would bring change.

....

There is very little laughter, except at his
hallucinations.
Speaking to concrete cat pillars on a come-down
like pets.
Naming them:
Lila
Lupin
Laila

Even that laughter covers the preceding terror
of the next round of the fight.

The calls were

more dramatic toward the end.

I have tried to kill myself

Please call me

I have been stabbed

Please call me

I have crashed the car, going to jail, don't worry.

. . . .

Now the terror of saving him again.

With vodka I tried to level him out, ever the nurse

Measuring ounces of how much was just enough

To not get thrashed by his tongue.

. . . .

I became a workaholic, volunteer-aholic,

write-aholic, binge-watching addict.

Anything to numb myself from the devil

in my life.

I was good at it, and that saved ME.

Preserved me in some way—in a separate bottle.

God, work, service, writing, resting

....

7 times she said.

That's how many times it takes to leave a trauma
marriage.

It took me 2 times.

2 times was hard enough

....

And I made moments.

I wanted to believe that love was real

That I knew enough to marry at 26.

Marry someone in active addiction where

I became a sober target

The times I went for years without drinking

For my spiritual reasons,

Not wanting him to relapse reasons,

Enjoying my moral compass reasons.

You think you are better bitch

You think you are a saint bitch

You are a slut bitch

You have had abortions

Slept with men. men. men.

Your family are white trash

....

The same denigrating script

He would not remember

That he read to me with liquid pride

Trying to shred the light in me

I was an awful person back at him

I lashed back

Desperate

Disgusting

Dying slowly

Addiction does this to you

....

I wanted to drive over you,

then reverse over you again.

With a large truck.

Then I had to forgive you.

The rage felt amazing.

So did the forgiveness.

I opened my heart.

He took from it.

It felt good

Until he took too much.

Note to self: do not write blank checks.

Ever.

What was it about him that you loved?

It came to me.

It was my spiritual life.

He hooked me with that.

He spoke of great mysteries

I was trying to figure out.

I thought we were going

to walk on this path together

so I said "I DO, TILL I DIE."

....

And each time I was just a trash can in a corner,

He would fill me up with some words about

God in the moments of no chaos, the middle of the

storm.

I did worship man over God.

I was told that you should follow your husband

by God.

Eph 5:22

God writes, with layers. His Word.

I wanted to take them seriously: my vows.

So I scoured the Bible

Cor 7:11

"But if she does leave him"

There it was—I could. I did.

....

I left

For the first time.

The second time.

....

My years of chaos subsided
as our faces touched.
Your soft breath landed on me.
In that moment you changed me.
You needed to be adored and protected,
so I finally gave you what I needed,

I left him—for us.

Cherry-lipped, moon-eyed girl.

You are so gentle; I am jealous.

You make me forget how cynical

I am about all of life and love.

....

My delight:

You will always know that I delight in your presence.

I want you to see my eyes light up when you walk

into a room.

I want you to know that you are loved just because

you exist.

We sat in court.

Waiting for the judge.

I was relieved,

feeling overwhelmed by the 10 years

of life I believed was going to work.

And while dealing with all these complex emotions,

he says,

my soon-to-be EX husband says,

I'm so hard right now.

My soon-to-be unavailability turning him on.

Psychopath

Psychopath

Did I mention he is a psychopath.

Only because he did threaten to kill me.

Not once in his mind. To friends, family.

I wished he was dead, a few times too.

Never hired a hit man though.

It was the desperation of hating his disease,

again back to the 6-year-old me.

....

This is a highly complex human being,

and entirely shallow.

With a mask of sanity.

A book saved me. As I flipped through the pages,

because I read so fast, I wept so fast because now I

knew why I had been in this.

I found peace—for her sake. He was her father.

I had to.

What was good in all of this time?

Always God's Grace.

Her little arrival.

My tribe.

Laughter.

Writing.

Time away by myself.

And there are still memories now

as I work through the ashes of those 10 years ...

....

I tried our first holiday together.

We flew to Sri Lanka.

You can see it coming, the chaos.

It starts to waft up like a familiar smell

at the same pace each time.

Him wanting to go out and please

the crowds as a DJ,

off to another town with his music.

Leaving me alone in a foreign country.

Until I get the please call me phone call.

This time it's from the driver.

Desperate to offload

his dangerous passenger

who is hanging with junkies at a beach.

Bring him to me.

Forgetting that he shouted and
threatened me so loudly at the
reception when he returned
I asked for my own room and locked
myself inside because I was so scared

And I post photos of our holiday.
The sun, the ocean, my toes.

Not the terror.

Empty vodka bottle

staring at your friend filled with ash.

He was trying to fill his lonely holes with booze and

cigarettes last night.

And left at midnight for a whore.

How much longer could I do this?

I write this now,
with great compassion
for the women who did all of this.
But mostly I think she is stupid.
Because she is intelligent.

I almost don't recognize myself.

. . . .

Only 5 years out and I have
Made a start
To learn the alphabet
Normal
Calm
Respect

Celebrating in between with a 2 year bender of red
wine and cheap vodka.

It was my time now, my time.
Wrong celebration. It landed me in rehab.
It's normal as a trauma survivor,
But it caused more agony.
Finally I could be free

on my knees.

. . . .

In groups I knew what denial was, I saw the addict
who was likely to relapse again, I understood the
damages that the wives endure. That crack and
women are part of the illness. The same illness I had
inherited.

Yet another baton handed to me.

Bipolar, Addict, Trauma Survivor.

I think my threshold has been reached.

It was time for the normal curve.

I had a lot of practice to do.

HOPE

She changed me when I gave birth.

She turned into my hope.

Hope, myself and our new life together.

The trauma is gone.

I remember the funny fights—

The ones we had about toothpaste—

You squeezed from the bottom;

I squeezed from the top.

....

I always wanted to paint you a picture,

but my mind was tired.

I wanted you to

place your forehead against mine

so I could share what I saw.

The last few months:

I would cook you dinner and leave little notes

that I would give you a massage.

Then complain I was too tired when you asked for it.

Divorce

Is a badge you wear forever.
It says failure.
It says we did not work.

It says freedom.

She's a freedom fire.

You never told me that when I started stitching
myself up, it would feel like I was giving birth to
barbed wire.

Healing

The flowers on my desk watched me:

For a moment I forgot the pain.

No one had sent me flowers for pain before.

They will again—when I am dead.

Divorce Sunflowers

He was aggressive and I was kind.

I kept thinking he would change,

but his fire would never feel my wind.

Covers, keep me hidden for days
in a gray haze where I can't move.
Force pen to paper or paint to brush.
I know that will be good for me,
but I can't move.

My limbs need too much of my mind to
actually work.

Major depression.

You keep me up.

You keep me even.

You keep me calm.

You keep me sane.

Four little pills.

Waiting for this storm to end,
watching the sky burst into tears,
while I grasp at the dark colors
of the rainbow in my heart.

....

There's batshit crazy in me.
It makes people run toward me.

Many also run away.

"Your laugh is the best thing about you."

Forever my favorite compliment.

You keep reposting

that photo!!

Of you and our daughter

in the bath

when she was only little,

not noticing me half-naked in the mirror

with the camera.

An eternal moment of my entire marriage: Invisible.

Second to the Addict Demon.

We laugh now.

The constant tension is

unraveling into joy.

Do you feel like a mom?

No I feel like myself.

With a little personal entertainer.

....

Is it hard to be a single mom?

Yes.

A bad marriage is a lot harder.

You are gone.

The bed is so big and empty without you.

I love the space.

Throw your life into a sieve …

let all the

sediment,

shame,

sadness,

serenity,

sex,

sincerity,

secrets,

fall to the ground as you unravel.

God and I were chatting.

I told Him I was drinking too much.

He said: Try and stop.

His advice is always simple.

I'm the complication.

I tried to relive my lost teen years.

I kissed a guy on a beach.

I drank too much.

I kissed a guy on a couch.

I drank too much.

I had two marriage proposals, and my head hurt.

Slowly, you invited me to trust your palms.

Holding hands is something I never did.

Now I am like a greedy teenager.

Searching for someone to hold my hand.

………………

He gently asked if he could touch my braid.

Weird and cute.

A different kind of foreplay.

He obviously has a hair fetish.

God—I may need some help down here

Moderation—
she does not visit.
So I moved in with
Severe Moderation.

………………

I asked him
to remove
all the alcohol
from my hotel room.
He looked at me.
He wanted to ask why.
I just don't want to
sleep in a bar tonight.

QUIT

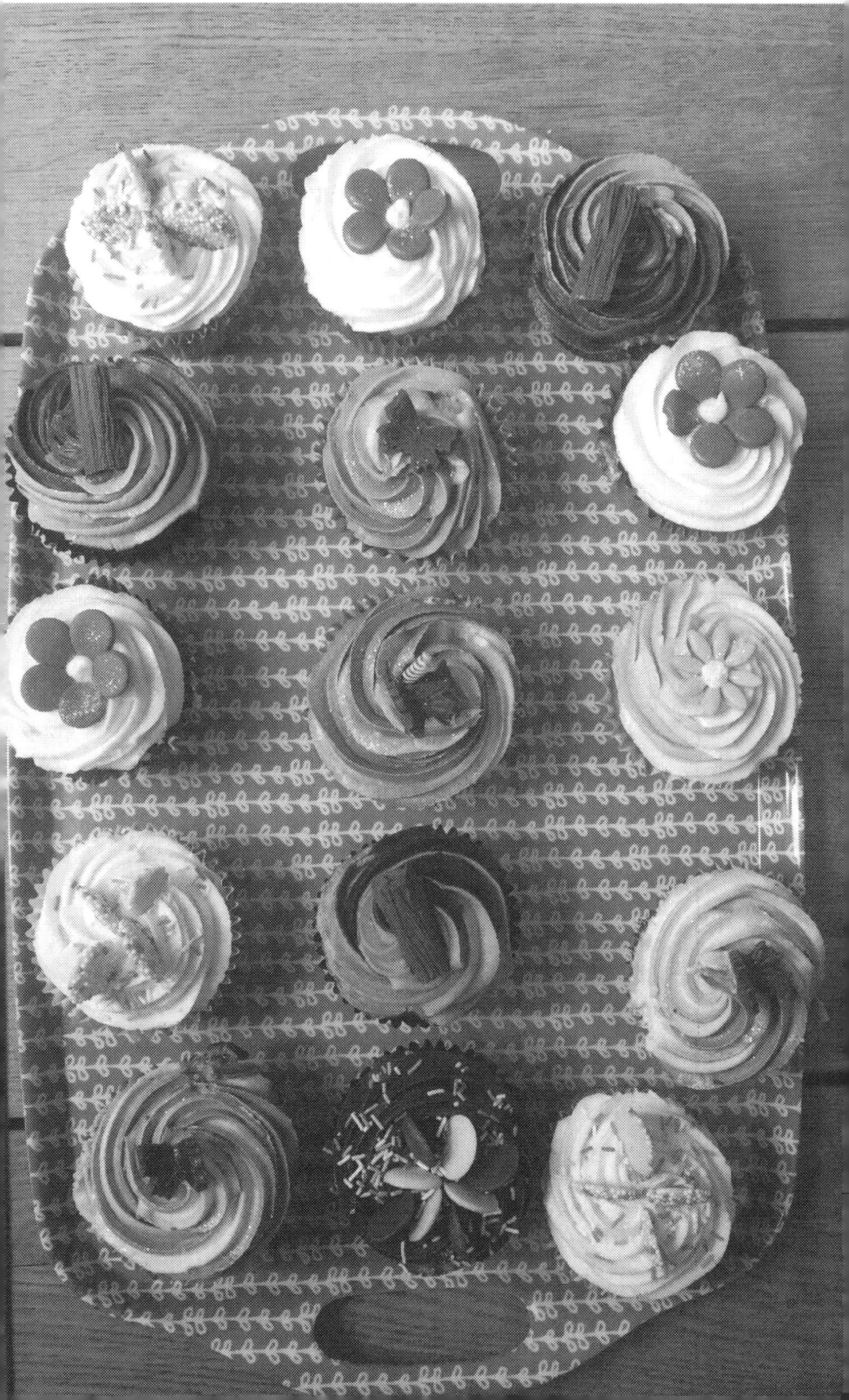

Excessively angry.

In passionate pursuit.

I raged a lot, always excessive, always passionate.

There were days I had to smile—

while I was choking to death.

Dealing with what I was dealt.

....

Suddenly my life made no sense.

The uncertain world we once shared was gone.

10 years of nothing—haunting me,

Had to work through the guilt
that came with
"Till death do us part."

Realized I had died inside.
So that settled it.

………………

My intolerable moods I have to hide from the world.
Suffering inside.
To me, I am just living.

Then I realize it's a lot for me;
I am only little.

I only miss you when

I have to take the cats to the vet.

Their boxes are too heavy

for me to lift alone.

Now they have been adopted.

I don't need you.

Courage, help me onto your shoulders.

What makes you tick?

Do all of it. Often.

So that when the sun sets in your eyes,

the unseen that keeps you in motion

will let it rise again.

Snooze button.
Snooze button.

Trying to will myself to live.

Snooze button.
Snooze button.

Latte and perhaps a Xanax.
I do hate you morning people.

My little one wanted to watch TV.
I told her to play with her toys.

She said she was tired and her
imagination was not working.

"Did you bond with your baby at birth?"

No, I passed out at the thought of them slicing open my womb.

I think she's okay.

There are days

when I realize

why my mother

was drunk

all the time.

Listening to incessant questions

from a toddler is much more fun

in a haze.

....

Mommy: my hero and my villain.

Raised us alone,

taught me that chaos was normal.

Trying to undo so much of it,

thirty-five years later.

Threads of inappropriateness,

innuendos in conversations
in what she said, he said, they said.

Generations keeping this sex stuff a total mess.
#metoo

My calm face
often hides a hellfire.

That dress—it's very accessible

Your words—she may find flattering,
for me they just painted a "no entry" sign.

Honesty invokes honesty.

It's a circle of love in my world.

You, single. It's unfair.

I watch you frown,

free and young,

lying there in charcoal gray,

that cute crease on your forehead

annoying me.

I'm jealous you can sleep until 2:00 p.m. on a
Saturday.

. . . .

He kissed me.

Then I heard the music,

a love song.

I turned it off.

The moment was way too *Titanic*.

You can
let your hair down
sober.

You just have to
take out your hair tie.

Two years sober

I wanted to say: *Shall we go for a drink to celebrate?*

Lush.

Fresh.

Our daughter.

My editor changed "my daughter" to "our daughter"

"That is so tragic that
your dad shot himself!"

Spilling 2.5 ounces
of expressed
breast milk on my first try
was way more tragic

....

I don't know how I landed up with a perfect child.
Her personality is handmade by God,
not my genes.

She reset me

Taught me gentle

Taught me tough

Taught me soft

....

My divorced bed is delighted

when filled

with a sleepover explosion of

mermaids

unicorns

insects

owls

feet

little eyelashes—closed,

dreaming of more playing.

She's a river of all of herself.

Shame

Is a bastard
who jails you in a dark cell.
If he just slid off your tongue, he'd be gone.

. . . .

I still get anxious
that Mom
will scream at me for writing
about her being drunk
my entire childhood.

Which part of me is still the young girl
afraid to bring a friend home?

Many have tough stories that need to be released to a kind ear.

You share.

You are strikingly honest.

You live gratitude.

Stop being so nice.

There is always some not so nice in us.

....

There is beauty in your

crudeness.

How could that be true?

Filth and finesse are divided?

Your kindness is wrapped in asshole.

PTSD

I spiraled into a descent,

into a pit inside my psyche,

trying to battle with myself.

And everyone said,

why would you

crash from an unwanted kiss?

....

I was in a version of hell

that you had no idea about.

Then you sent me a text:

"Are you fixed yet?"

So random, so weird, so right.

You were there.

Big compared to all the other small, sad people.

Pulling out my chair at breakfast.

It took me twenty-one days to trust you.

Then you kissed me goodbye.

A vile kiss broke me; your kiss helped me get well.

Rehab kiss

Flames teased my cheeks
as he pulled me closer.

....

It took time to get well.

Time I can't explain.

Since I lost my memory.

....

You stroked my hair,

told me I reminded you of the kind of woman
you liked,

that I was the most adorable girl in the world.

Sometimes I go back

Into that rage

Of the time you stole from me

Yes or no

You just needed to ask for the kiss.

Disdain covers your kindness.

People need to work hard to know you.

Make it easier.

You won't be so alone.

....

He cried.

The sadness spilt onto his cheeks.

The relief was fleeting; I watched the hurt return.

Refused any help, so next time he cried,

I changed the subject.

Crack this coconut

hard, on your head.

Let it bleed and swell,

hoping reality

might envelop you.

Pain just falls off you.

Can we settle this divorce already.

You fell for my yoni.

For you, it was love.

When you found out I was seeing someone,

you were jealous—

an old Tantra master wanting all my heat to himself.

Did some weird stuff in my twenties.

I have encountered you, darkness,

for years, but only mildly.

Maybe once unable to get out

of bed for seven days.

This time I crashed into a hole;

it seemed it would last forever.

I did not have that amount of

time,

so I started to move upward,

one inch at a time.

16 months—Postnatal Depression

My brain burns.
Begging silently
for deprivation
or overconsumption.

It's so quiet
I have to ask others:
can you hear it?

....

I read your book. It was about clawing through a
broken heart to peace.
I could relate to the clawing.
I knew no other language.*

*Classifieds: Seeking a language tutor.

Belly-ring

I put you back in.

Perhaps to escape

back to being 20.

Two decades ago—

crazy free.

Or perhaps

I want your sparkle

to remind me

that I birthed a miracle.

The Bed for Her.

Feelings could not form words.

We made love to make up for that.

You needed to talk.

She could do that.

You changed your apartment around for her.

We made love in the bed you bought for her—

your last attempt to see if I would speak.

....

I love you, he said.

What must I do with that? I replied.

What is your morbid fascination with not getting

attached to me?

Just accept that I love you, woman.

It did go undone—he was too young.

Christ

All the roundabouts sending me spinning.
Your caress always just around the corner.

I woke up to a death threat.

The same day you said you loved me for the
first time.

I will kill you.

I will love you.

It was a complex day.

Single

I am trying this thing of wrapping myself in myself.
I am getting it right.
I am also getting
involved,
infatuated,
distracted.

....

Orphan

I traced a line of sugar
across the orange sky.
It led my hand to Pluto.
I want to hold you,
unimportant one.

I thought I was average.

She said no.

You, my dear,

are an overcomer

of tremendous mountains.

A mountaineer?

I hate climbing.

It's easy to put on a disguise,

Glow All Out Powder,

Bahama Mama Bronzer,

High Beam Highlighter.

To the world, I can always look fresh.

....

You looked into my eyes and saw beyond the
face paint.

Reached over and gave me
the cuddle I needed.

Perhaps today,
I could do with
someone gentle.
Beside or
beneath me.

....

I can only remember your kisses.

I wonder if you also touched her soul
with your mouth
the way you did mine.

My solitude,

me and all of myself.

So very bored today.

I was out of his league.

I concluded I was a conquest,

so I let him conquer.

....

I stood in the sunlight.
He looked at me.
I wanted him to see me.
He got hard,
the moment was lost.

Lust, you loser.

Your hands in me.

My body had stopped working,

until your words reached me.

I knew my body needed a talking to.

Come on—say that again.

I prayed for compassion;
I went through judgment.
I prayed for forgiveness;
I was betrayed.
I prayed for wisdom;
I was given challenges.
I prayed for kindness;
I was faced with cruelty.

You have no purpose,

Except to let the sun reach earth.

After I dropped my marriage burden,
I felt elated.
My friends said they could see it in my eyes.

Could also be the antidepressants.

You fetched me a lily in a swamp,

walked to me with fresh mud on your shoes.

You handed it to me

in front of a crowd—so brave:

I liked that you got dirty for me.

I fully exist as my true self

when we laugh together until we nearly wet

ourselves.

Space

and rest.

Important on paper and for life.

Tickles

Strawberries

Kisses

Blueberries

How do we become adults who just

Want

Want

Want

When berries and kisses are all we need

Those late-night phone calls to make me laugh.

They all thought we were in love.

It was just an aura of understanding.

....

He is not a man caught up in desire so much that he needs to consume or be consumed.

There is something deeply respectful in that: to allow a moment to exist without claiming or owning it.

In my dream, I lay on my left side.

I could almost feel your nose;
we were connected like two hands clasped.
I knew that my attachment
was far deeper than I let on.

My dreams are always my reality
that I sometimes won't admit.

CRUSH

You were playful.

You were protective.

You held my hand.

You picked me wildflowers.

A small mountain romance.

....

I've missed this flushed feeling.

I feel needed and naughty.

Then when I'm still,

I imagine what is beneath

this frivolous glow.

It's the feeling of leaning into someone.

So many years I've done this alone,

I don't even know what it feels like,

to lean into someone and feel safe.

I keep saying it's all okay

when I just want to

be held for two years.

Your touch scalds me and

soothes my sanity.

I watch the warmth return,

and I want you close forever

while I gaze at the burn marks

intently.

That was some hot lovemaking.

I tried this because I wanted you.

I was afraid of getting too close.

I ended up lying next to you naked,

looking at your striking profile.

Your eyes had no hurting in them.

I'm completely open with you.

I'm completely guarded with you.

Understand both exist within me.

Several times I tried.

Several times I failed.

I'll keep trying.

I like trying.

Keeps me out of trouble.

That's a lie.

I like being in trouble.

You said I smelled

like honey on a rainbow.

I wondered if it was rehearsed,

so I googled—but they were your words.

....

You lay on the bed, watched me intently.

I playfully twirled around,

stretching my arms up,

my gaze on you.

I wanted you to watch me, look right into my eyes.

I needed that: to be seen.

I cry with

gratitude,

love,

grief.

You said comfort comes in tears.

God.

Just laugh.

Everything looks better with a halo of laughter.

I woke with the fresh feeling of your caress.

Reached over, and my bed was empty.

The smell of your sky and the taste of your ocean

left me wishing I could be a tiny toy boat.

Free, so the currents could take me on their journey.

You cannot tell me not to believe.

Debate my faith:
how can faith be debated?

My tribe is truth.

My tribe is free.

My tribe is laughter.

. . . .

Tell me what

Disturbs you,

Disgusts you,

Drives you,

Delights you.

Restraint:

the space that
stops me
from behaving
like a lunatic.

I see that heavy mask you wear,

Your stars guarded by darkness.

I will love you and understand you,
Since you came to be that way through pain.

Your tongue—a sword of feelings stabbing my torso.

There is a yearning to be held.

I know that will not be eternal,

so I go back in prayer, and You hold me.

It's that promise You have kept for so many years.

Agape

Jab me with glass.

Leave scars in my flesh.

Try to change me. Tempt me. Hurt me.

You know I belong to God.

You cannot touch my faith

or my soul.

You get mad,

so you keep trying

with sweet seduction

and painful experiences.

You are relentless

with your beauty and pain.

I fell asleep, imagining you were holding me.

You gently lay on top of me,

feeling my thoughts with your chest.

Silent tears started to roll down my cheeks.

You kissed them away.

I was thinking of the time you lay on my lap

and said I looked pretty upside down.

....

Peace

My home is my sanctuary.

It is the most peaceful place.

Took me long enough to figure out this thing

called stillness.

Some days I don't want
to do this anymore.
Then You visit me
in a dream and
whisper in my ear:
Hold on, hold on.

Why do people pay for Life Coaches when God is free?

....

I want to be a generational cycle breaker

In parenting,
In relationships,
In living.

I forgot You in the pain.
Your faint voice was
clouded in the thunder.
I kept listening for the shout,
when Your answer
was a gentle whisper.

....

What I see is not real;
only You are.
I love You Lord,
but sometimes
I need a reminder.

Wash me.
Or drown me to remember.

I wanted him to have me,

to get this anger out,

then maybe hug.

If only my arms could fold.

....

I told him about

my wild twenties,

thinking he'd leave.

Except it made him want me more.

Sometimes you have to toss a coin on how much

truth you let out.

Every day is a fight to keep

electricity flowing in my veins.

I am tired; my brain feels fossilized.

I want to lie against your hair.

You can be anyone who smells nice.

Just not Issey Miyake—that makes me sneeze.

He was so proud of it.

You would think he'd be happy

and give the topic no thought,

but it was all he could talk about.

I liked everything else about him,

but I got bored of his obsession.

Manhood

My hand reached yours, and you touched me inside.
My body tightened, and I exhaled desire.

Inside I had years of tears.

Mercury and gravity collided,

and time broke for four seconds.

I screamed,

lost in my mind, watching profound words

that could not form a sentence,

caught between a high and a low.

Hypomania

Things are falling apart, seemingly, but I am okay,
I think.

Scared of that abyss I just desperately tunneled my
way out of.

He's interesting—I just saw it in
his eyes for a moment.

I wanted to try him.

"Can I talk to you?"

"**No**, I am dancing, and I can't multitask."

Another failed pickup line.

I do the approaching—you all make me feel vulnerable.

Left behind in the hills,

we walked for hours,

my nose cracked from the cold.

A daffodil bravely watched me

pick up a stone.

Why that souvenir?

What Next?

Maybe there is a light beyond,
or perhaps the universe
collapsed
in a place where we are suspended
to hold on to nothing.

How can you assume to know me?

Have you lived in my hips?

You're a puzzle.

With edges that don't fit together.

....

Then I found you.

We played. You called me monkey.

You said you had not met someone like me.

I have not met someone like me.

Panic, she gripped my being.

I was like ice.

Hugging my daughter, wishing she'd sleep.

The cave in my head was empty,

except for the days I could paint.

No one knew what it felt like to

be the only one stuck

in a body and mind

of iron while the rest of

the world was fluid.

My Little One

I am tired.
I ask you to close my door.
I tell you I am working.

It's a lie.

I worry that I might go

down,

down,

down,

and not be able to take care of you properly.

I am glad I have people who

love you when my limbs are too tired to hold you.

I thought my independence may be too heavy
for him.

His knees buckled, and he told me it was my fault.

I want to sit with you and make suicide jokes.

What do you do?

"It's 1:00 a.m.

I am pretty sure it's not my career you are

interested in."

The softness of spontaneity.

We jump together when we feel like it.

....

A kiss tells all.

Just your lips

will let me decide

if I will want you again.

There was a moment I held onto you.

We grew together,

our roots entwined tightly.

Then I ripped up the whole lot.

Your roots choked me.

Like an inquisitive boy stretching a live worm,
delighting in death while he fishes.

Those worms eat at my mind.

There is no delight in that.

Why on earth would you offer to carry me?

I carry myself.

Watch.

But occasionally my legs really hurt.

Lord?

I cannot find my hands in the dark, nor Yours.
Reach out to me and hold me.

....

I ran through my mind,
looking for the part that could swim
while my thighs were slowly sinking.

I told you, that stare just makes me want to lie with
you again.

I have to go to work.

I could call in sick?

SPACE

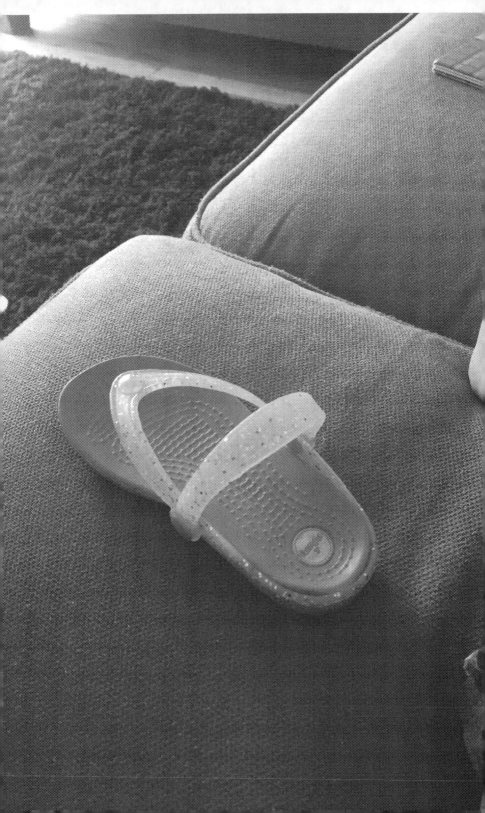

Black and yellow spiraled.

It was pain and freedom coming together,

trying to make sense of each other.

Black always won on my canvas. Why?

Painting gives me life.

....

I am just a big kid

Trying to raise another kid

Trying to grow up a year faster

than her

If I extinguished your hurt, you thought you would feel better.

You won't.

Your pain is not my pain.

I can only hold you while you hurt.

I sat in the sunlight scowling,

Trying to figure out if this mind

that raced like a rat on speed

was visible to the clouds.

Everyone says I am peaceful,

except you, sky.

You know my mania.

....

Mania is a seductress,

she lures you upwards

until she is satisfied with

her ingenious chaos.

Suddenly she discards you,

leaving you isolated,

praying on bruised knees.

I remember the first time

I was in a cinema.

With a man I loved,

doing a job I loved,

yet all I could do was worry.

Webster's said it was anxiety.

....

Hunched in the bath,

I sat sobbing,

tears mixed with bubbles,

asking God why it hurt.

He whispered: Make changes.

Of course, I did not listen.

I thought I knew better than the big man in the sky.

Present, striking, strong.

I wanted to feel that.

Then you combusted.

Just another person so engulfed in themselves.

Why is it that when I reach out with my arms you become invisible?

Mirror,

I see the same nine-year-old
who stared at you and wondered what
or who had made me.
Behind the flesh and reflection in my eyes,
there's a light that looks like a soul.

I lay with my back toward you.

I thought your hand on my hip was enough.

You wanted me to face you,

to drink from my eyelashes and cheeks.

Get drunk from me.

Please—I want you to.

. . . .

I held you in my mouth, or you held me.

You kissed the way I kiss.

Then I said I must go and I left.

I actually meant I wanted to stay.

. . . .

Man—with your soft words

Not trying to own me.

I like you.

You waited and waited
until I came to you.
I made you a meal.
You said I was perfect.
I left after dinner. No one is perfect.

....

He said he was really into me.
He asked me about my past.
It made him doubt.
He asked me about my present.
It made him doubt.
He asked me about my mind.
It made him doubt.
I don't think he's into me anymore.

How much of you will I tolerate?

I hear your faint lies falling as you try to win me over.

Be brave. Be real.

Not for me, for you.

I loved my cats as an adult.

They were my children,

until I forgot to feed them for weeks.

I loved babies as a teenager.

I was babysitting all the time,

until I started hating babies for weeks.

I realized I had a mood disorder way before I

thought I did.

God knows

I am twirling into a

spiritual descent.

I watch it like a tumbleweed,

and I know God can stop it.

I just need to want that.

There was adoration in your eyes

and mistrust.

Learn to trust me.

I will not destroy you while being adored.

Fool.

What does together feel like?

I want to be an *us*.

Together, so close that I don't have to search
for you.

He said he loved me.

He also said

he wondered what his friends would think about his

crazy wife if we got married.

He's the insane one.

. . . .

He asked,

"What would your life be like

if I helped you simplify it?"

I sobbed,

then kept going alone—I was not

looking for a knight.

You want me.

What is it?

I see it in your eyes.

There is nothing to me.

Or maybe everything?

Cocoon Baby

You want to be covered from head to toe,

sleeping in a pod of oblivion.

As I do with my arm across my face.

You snuggle, while I try to hide from the world.

Words drift around and settle.

Do you understand?

Me?

You?

Them?

That rosebud you put next to my bed.

It stares at me, testing if I will accept

someone to love me again.

Don't wilt, little rose.

Stay alive; I might accept you.

Or put you in a book and squash and dry you.

Letting Go

A deep ravine opened its mouth,
wanting to swallow and drown me,
or kiss me while I floated in bliss.
It was hard to tell from this side.

He was comforting.

Messaging me

something profound

or stupid.

It did not matter.

He was just always there, draining my iPhone
battery.

Insomnia.

Severe.

Unsure what would happen when you arrived.

Then you were in my arms.

I slept more than I had in weeks.

Everything the opposite of what new moms told me.

I guess my childhood training all came back to me.

Her feet are too large for her little body.

The proportions are wrong.

So perfect, my lanky toddler.

. . . .

My words want to come out,

all the crass and crude.

I keep it cool

so that when she reads it one day, her mom will be

honest but tempered.

I should pen some pretty poems.

Cherry blossoms falling in slow motion,

warm vanilla candles,

air that wraps me and smells of snow,

your dimples.

....

She thought I was so regular.

My wars were invisible to her,

so I went with regular.

It felt glorious to be just that.

I tried to explain she was three years old.

She kept protesting that she only had two ears.

. . . .

Your little cheeks, wrapped in my sheets.

A cherub princess, pure.

Then you fart.

Toilet Radar

She runs in,
spreads my legs
to watch the pee bubbles with delight.
It's endearing,
but mostly totally awkward.

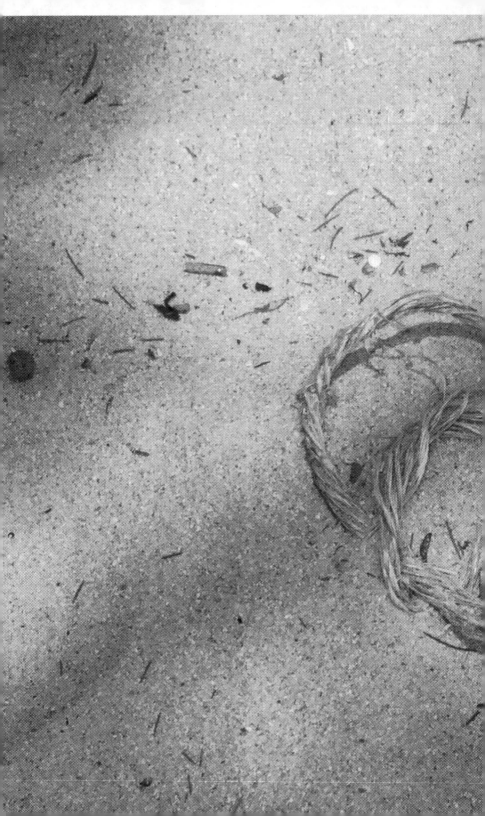

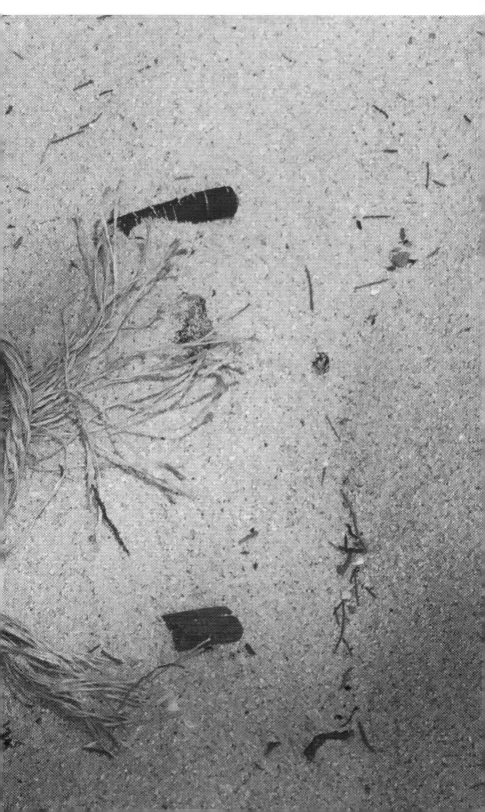

You never criticized or belittled me,

even when I drowned in mistakes.

You helped me undo the loud screams

that echoed in my mind my entire life.

One day it occurred to me: they had become

a small whisper.

Clouds reach down.

Let me float in your mist

so I can be invisible today.

Mom holiday needed.

Journals

To let memories

Evaporate,

Dissipate,

Disseminate,

Dismantle my mind.

"There are nine planets."

"No, Mummy, there are only eight."

When did I lose track of the universe?

She spritzed my plant,
Touched its leaves tenderly
with her little hands,
Told the little fella to grow
And to make more lilies.

Might have swallowed one of my pills?

Smell my breath, Mom.

Smell my hands, Mom.

Smell my hair, Mom.

She likes her life to smell good

And tells me when I smell bad.

I wake up at 7:00 a.m.

I don't want the day to exist.

I go to sleep at 10:00 p.m.,

my heart imploding with gratitude.

Rapid cycling.

Parenting One Day

Legs across me.

Breathing next to me.

You've always wanted to be intertwined.

Touching, tickling, tactile.

My lovely baby, the one I want to inhale.

Parenting Another Day

You are a never-ending project with no deadline.

I am too tired for this.

I need a vacation—
without you.

Runs out of my room, screaming my songs are
too sad.
So I put on her playlist.

Some are sad too, but her sadness sounds different.

....

You hear me on the phone,
angry about something at work,
and you say, "Please, Mummy, don't use that voice!"

Parenting me.

That memory:
Mom was drunk again,
trying to do CPR on me.

I was lying very still
in our garden,
on my back,
trying to stop a nosebleed.

I was not dead. I was seven.

Mom,
your "I love you"
sounds like your "leave me alone"
tonight.

The journals
Turned into poetry
A manuscript
A Book

....

It hurt inside
I realized I was selling
the intimate words of my life.

I got over it in a day.

I have to write.
Words are the residue of my world.

I was rehearsing lines.
Returned to
class, my neck in a spasm.
I could not do my lines.
Burst into tears.
I had gone so far into
character.
A woman fearing she
was crazy.

I had to play myself.

Left Hollywood.

Eventually every

scream,
scar,
bruise,
beating,
tear,
torment,

brought me some form of beauty.

....

Show me
a woman
stronger
than one
who has
rebuilt
her own jungle
some bastard
trampled on.

A Little
Appendix:

**Exquisite Thoughts from
My Existentialist Five-Year-Old**

Mommy how did God hang the whole sky?

....

Sadness is in my heart.
Then it comes up
all the way to my eyes.
It's okay; it will go away.

One day the toilet will swallow me,

and I will never escape.

Unless I am too big for its throat.

....

After staring at the trees, she turned to me.

"I think the trees are very tired.

They have been standing for a very long time."

Please can we ask God to turn all the racists into
good people?

. . . .

No one is allowed to make you feel scared.
I was TERRIFIED mommy, not scared.

She reminds me to find my fight.

. . . .

Be a cuddly octopus
trapped inside a human toy
and wrap around me

I stared at the mirror, and all I saw was glass.

....

If I think about happy things I am happy.

....

God must have a lot of work if He has to look after the whole world.

....

Mommy how long can I stay small for? Big people need to do a lot and I want to be small for a long time.

This book was partially edited on a cracked iPhone wrapped in Sellotape.

Thank you, AB.